Annie Makes a Big Change

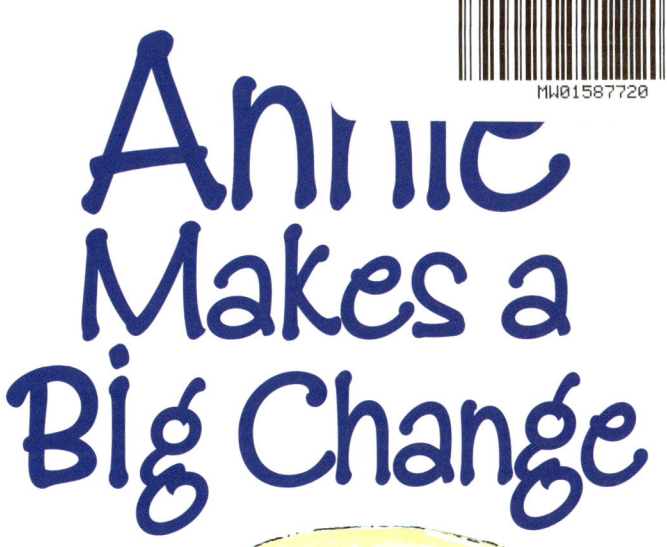

by John Manos
illustrated by Janice Fried

Scott Foresman
is an imprint of

Glenview, Illinois • Boston, Massachusetts • Chandler, Arizona
Upper Saddle River, New Jersey

Illustrations
Janice Freid

Photographs
Every effort has been made to secure permission and provide appropriate credit for photographic material. The publisher deeply regrets any omission and pledges to correct errors called to its attention in subsequent editions.

Unless otherwise acknowledged, all photographs are the property of Pearson Education, Inc.

16 ©Steve Gorton/Getty Images

ISBN 13: 978-0-328-51352-9
ISBN 10:   0-328-51352-0

Copyright © by Pearson Education, Inc., or its affiliates. All rights reserved.
Printed in the United States of America. This publication is protected by copyright, and permission should be obtained from the publisher prior to any prohibited reproduction, storage in a retrieval system, or transmission in any form or by any means, electronic, mechanical, photocopying, recording, or likewise. For information regarding permissions, write to Pearson Curriculum Rights & Permissions, One Lake Street, Upper Saddle River, New Jersey 07458.

Pearson® is a trademark, in the U.S. and/or in other countries, of Pearson plc or its affiliates.

Scott Foresman® is a trademark, in the U.S. and/or in other countries, of Pearson Education, Inc., or its affiliates.

8 9 10 11 V010 17 16 15 14 13

Annie felt wonderful as she walked to the bridge across the stream. The sky overhead was blue. The sun felt warm. Fall was Annie's favorite season. She liked to see the leaves changing colors.

Then Annie heard the sound of machines. Workers were cutting down the trees near the stream!

Annie was very mad. She did not know what was happening, but she would soon find out.

The next day, Annie's mother showed her the newspaper. It had a story about the trees. They were being cut down to clear the land. Some people wanted to build new houses by the stream.

"This is unfair," Annie said. "That land should be a park!"

"Let's not complain," said Annie's mother. "What can we do to solve this problem?"

Annie turned away with a shrug. "I don't know."

"I know that the land belongs to Mrs. Potter," said Annie's mother. "Maybe we can talk to her."

Annie was afraid of Mrs. Potter. She was old, and kids at school said she was mean. They said that she mumbled at kids. Still, Annie knew that she would have to talk to Mrs. Potter if she wanted to save the trees.

Annie asked her mother to go with her to see Mrs. Potter. They saw Mrs. Potter through the window. She looked unhappy. Annie was brave and knocked on the door.

The door opened. "Yes?" Mrs. Potter asked.

Annie wanted to disappear. She could not talk.

"Yes?" Mrs. Potter said again.

Finally, Annie spoke. As she explained about the trees and the stream, Mrs. Potter began to nod.

"You want my land to be part of a park," Mrs. Potter guessed. When Annie said yes, Mrs. Potter said, "Then we need to get to work." They both smiled.

"We will need to get people to help us," Mrs. Potter said. "We will need many signatures from people who agree with us. We will ask the people in charge of the town to make a park. We can get people to vote about the park."

How to Make a Big Change

"We can do that?" Annie asked.

"Of course we can," Annie's mother answered.

"How do we do it?" Annie wondered.

Mrs. Potter smiled again. "You will see, but I hope you like walking," she said.

How to Make a Big Change

See and write about a problem.
When you want to change something big, you need to ask public officials to help you. You need to write on a paper what you want to change. Be sure to include details. This is called a petition.

Get signatures.
Show other people the petition. If they agree with you, they will sign their names. Each person can only sign once.
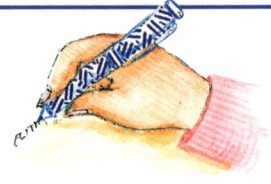

Show public officials your petition.
Someone will check the signatures.

Public officials decide what to do next.
What will happen depends on many things.

All through the fall, Annie and her mother walked from door to door. Annie asked people to sign her petition. She was always very nice. She did not want to annoy anyone. Some days, she didn't want to go. But she always made herself go. She kept asking people to sign.

Annie even asked the workers at the stream for signatures.

"Get out of here!" one man shouted.

Annie wanted to cry. Then three other workers told her they would sign her petition. They made her feel much better.

Finally, she had all of the signatures she needed. Annie and Mrs. Potter gave the petition to the town officials. They told Annie and Mrs. Potter that people could vote about the park in the spring.

At last, the day of the vote arrived. Mrs. Potter came to Annie's house to wait for the news.

The voting was not over until 7:00 P.M. Then the votes were counted. Annie could hardly stand the waiting! She fell asleep without knowing what would happen.

In the morning, Mom's big smile told Annie what she wanted to know. The city would redo the land to make a new park! She knew Mrs. Potter would be happy too.

Before the next fall, the park was ready. Annie loved to see her friends playing on the new playground. People sat on new benches next to the stream to look at the fall colors. Even Mrs. Potter joined in the fun!

Get Involved

Getting signatures on a petition is not the only way to make things better. Here are two more ideas.

Make less garbage. You can recycle almost everything. Recycle means to use something again. Glass, metal, paper, and plastic can all be recycled.

Give some of your time. Animals in a shelter may need you to visit. They may need baths or a walk. Town gardens may need cleaning. Older people might need help in their yards.

There are many things you can do to make things better. It will make you feel good too!